# Chin Music

# Also by Alvin Schwartz

# Chin Music

## TALL TALK and OTHER TALK

Collected from American Folklore
by **ALVIN SCHWARTZ**
Illustrated by JOHN O'BRIEN

J. B. Lippincott / New York

J
427.9
S

*Library of Congress Cataloging in Publication Data*

Schwartz, Alvin, n. d.  Chin Music.
Bibliography: p.
SUMMARY: Presents examples of folk speech used
during the period 1815 to 1950. Identifies their meaning
and the regions in which they were collected.
1. Americanisms—Juvenile literature.
2. English language—Slang—Juvenile literature.
3. English language—Terms and phrases—Juvenile
literature. 4. Words, New—English—Juvenile literature. 5. Folklore—United States—Juvenile literature. [1. Americanisms. 2. English language—Slang.
3. English language—Terms and phrases. 4. Folklore—
United States] I. O'Brien, John, n. d.    II. Title.
PE2846.S36    427'.9'73    79-2403
ISBN 0-397-31869-3   ISBN 0-397-31870-7 lib. bdg.
ISBN 0-397-31871-5 pbk.

2   4   6   8   9   7   5   3   1

For

**M.E.M.**

# Contents

# Horse Fly!

When an old man I know is feeling really gloomy he says, "Oh, I have the dismals!" But when he's feeling really happy he calls out, "Horse fly!"

One time I asked him where he got these sayings. He said he learned them from other people when he was a boy. "They were just passed around and handed down," he said.

All the old words and sayings in this book are like that. Nobody ever learned them at school. People just made them up when they needed a good way of saying what was on their minds.

They might think about how something looked or sounded or behaved, or what it reminded them of. Then they'd make up a word based on that. Or they'd take a word they already knew and fix it up the way they wanted it.

That's how they made up "whoopity-scoot," "argufy," "gollybuster," "glopsloptious," "smooched up," and the other words and sayings in this book.

If a word turned out to be useful, their neighbors began using it. And it was passed around and handed down until a better word came along.

11

When that old man was growing up, people spent a lot of their free time sitting around and talking and telling stories—"making chin music," they called it.

These old words and sayings they used made for a lot of good talk and a lot of good times. Just try them, and you'll never be hog-tied when it comes to making chin music.

ALVIN SCHWARTZ

Princeton, New Jersey

# WORDS
### and
# SAYINGS

## Angry, Mad

Dudfoozled. "I was just dudfoozled. I was mad enough to bite stumps. I was mad enough to eat needles."

## Animals

Varmints.

See Bear, Dog, Galliwampus, Panther, Skunk, Snake, Snallygaster.

## to Annoy, to Bother

To dingdong. "Now behave yourself! Don't you dingdong that child again. Just let him be."

## to Argue

To argufy. "It's no use. argufyin' the matter. I *am* the ugliest man on earth. Thar's narry 'nuther like me."

## Arithmetic

To add: To sumtotalize.

To subtract: To subtotalize.

# B

## Bald-headed Man

Onion-head.

## Banjo

Box. Groundhog.

## Banjo Player

Box knocker.
Groundhog beater.

## Bear

B'ar.

B'ar story:

One day when Oak Wing's sister was goin' to a baptizin', she seed this big b'ar come out of a holler tree. She had her dinner with her in a paper bag, and the b'ar looked at the dinner and looked at her as if he didn't know which to eat fust.

Well, she stood a minute and stared at him in hopes he would feel ashamed of hisself an' go away. But he just poked out his nose and smelled of the dinner—which

war sassengers made of b'ar meat and crocodile liver—
and then he smelt of her.

When he did that, she threw the dinner down before
him. And when he put his nose to it, she jumped on top
of him and sunk her teeth into the scruff of his neck. As
her teeth war long and sharp as nails, he shot ahead like
a cannonball. But she held on, and her teeth stripped the
coat right off him, clear down to the tail. A week later
that b'ar was seen up in Muskrat Holler runnin' around
naked as he was born. Oak Wing's sister, she made
herself a good warm petticoat out of that pesky varmint's
hide.

# BIG ANIMAL OR PERSON

Gollybuster. Gollywhopper.

## to Boast

To shoot off your bazoo.

## Boastful Person

Mouth-almighty.

## Boasts and Brags

See Tall Talk.

## the Body

See Bald-Headed Man, Eyes, Face, Feet, Hand, Knees, Legs, Mouth, Nose, Stomach, Teeth, Throat.

## Bogeyman

Boogeroo. Willipus-wallipus. "If you don't watch out, the boogeroo will get you, and if he doesn't the willipus-wallipus will."

## to be Brave

To be full of sand. To have sand on your gizzard. "He was just plumb full of sand—had enough for a whole lakefront."

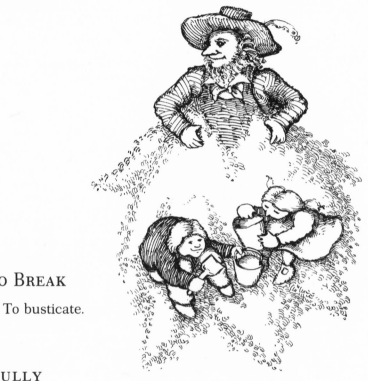

## to Break

To busticate.

## Bully

Killcow.

## Bullet

Lead pill.
Also see Gun.

# C

### BE CALM

Don't fret your pups.

### TO CHEAT

To hocus. "Don't let him hocus you. He'll do it every time if you don't watch out."

### CLOTHES

See Dressed Up, Fancy Clothes, Hat.

### CLUMSY PERSON

Gollumpus. Gump.

## COMPLETELY, TOTALLY

Teetotaciously. "They have teetotaciously ruinated everything."

## CONCEITED, STUCK UP

Biggity.

## CONCEITED PERSON

Fuddle-britches.

## CONFUSED

Betwaddled. Bumfuzzled. Golumgumtiated. "After the mare throwed me, I was so bumfuzzled I couldn't tell wet from windy."

## A COOK

Bean master. Dough belly. Gut robber.

## COWARD

Clam-face. Possum.

# D

## to Dance

To shake a hoof. To sling an ankle. "My sister slings the nastiest ankle in town."
Also see Party.

## THE DARK

"It was as dark
as a stack
of black cats."
"It was so dark
she couldn't
hear herself
talk."

## DELICIOUS

Glopsloptious.
"This strawberry
pie is just
glopsloptious."

## Dentist

Tooth carpenter.

## Dirty

Boongy (pronounced boon-jee).

## Dishonest

"He was so crooked he had to screw his socks on."

## DIZZY

"He was so dizzy he had to hold on to the grass before he could lean against the ground."

## DOCTOR

Pillroller.

## Dog

Bone-cruncher.

## Dressed Up

Slicked up. Smooched up. Triggered out. "He got all triggered out in his Sunday suit. He was dressed up like a sore toe."

# E

## EATING TALK

Hungry: "My belly thinks my throat is cut." "My tongue is hanging out a foot and forty inches."

Eating: Putting on the nose bag.

Eating together: Messing together.

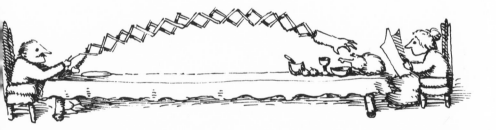

Let's eat: "Make long arms!" "Take and rake!"

Have another helping: "Fill your shirt!"

Eating too much: Padding out your belly.

Also see Food and Drink, Restaurant.

## EMBARRASSED

Puckerstoppled.

## TO ESCAPE

To save your bacon.

## EVERYDAY TALK

Chin music. Jawbation. "He is never hog-tied when it comes to makin' chin music. His tongue is just plumb frolicsome."

## Exactly

Prezactly. "When he seed he warn't prezactly dead, he felt all over to make sure all of him was still there."

## Excited

All a-twitter. Excited as a cat at a mouse show.

## Eyes

Lookers.

## Eyeglasses

Cheaters.

# F

## FACE

Osfrontis. "To read a man you only have to look at his osfrontis."

## FANCY CLOTHES

Fumadiddle.

## FAST

Lickety-toot. Lickety-whoop. Whoopity-scoot. "He ate his supper lickety-whoop, then whoopity-scoot he ske-daddled into town."

# FAT

Poundiferous.

Story about a poundiferous girl:

This boy had a girl friend who was so poundiferous he could only hug one part of her at a time. So when he called on her he always had a piece of chalk with him. He would hug as much of her as he could, then mark the place, then hug her again. But once when he had gotten halfway around, he met a fellow coming around the other side.

## Feet

Clod-knockers.


## to Fib, to Lie, to Make Up Stories

To woof someone. "I figured she was a-woofin' me about her trip to the big city."
Also see Lying.


## Fierce, Ferocious

Riprocious. Savage as a meat-ax. "So I went over there savage as a meat-ax, strutting around, making faces, scaring everybody in sight."

## Fighting Talk

A fight: Bustification. Squabblification.

Fighters: Scrougers. "Those gals warn't any of your pigeon creatures, but real scrougers. Any one of 'em could lick a b'ar easy."

A punch in the mouth: A pat on the lip.

A punch in the nose: A shuck in the snoot.

A really hard punch, a knockout blow: Ferricadouzer. Sockeroo. "So I rushed in and with great force planted a ferricadouzer smack on his smeller."

To beat somebody up: To blotterate, to chaw up, or exfluncate someone. To hang up his or her hide. To obfliscate, or rumsquaddle him or her. "I really blotterated him. When I finished, he was obfliscated, exfluncated, rumsquaddled, and chawed up. I just hung up his hide."

Rough-and-tumble: When two people had a fistfight in the old days, that was called a "fair fight." But on the frontier or in the backwoods, now and then they went a lot further. Someone might kick his opponent or try to bite off one of his ears or part of his nose, or even try to gouge out one of his eyes. They called that "rough-and-tumble with no holds barred."

A rough-and-tumble rhyme:

>They fit and fit and gouged a bit
>And struggled in the mud
>Until the ground for miles around
>Was kivered with their blood.
>And a pile of noses, ears, and eyes,
>Large and massive, reached the skies.

Also see Tall Talk.

## to Flatter

To sweet-mouth. "He sweet-mouthed me all day, but it didn't get him anywhere."

## Food and Drink

Biscuits: Cat heads. Snowballs.
Big biscuits: Belly-breakers.
Butter: Cow paste.
Coffee: Jangle juice.
Eggs: Hen apples.
Gelatin salad: Nervous salad.
Gravy: Goozlum.
Ham: Grunt.
Honey: Bee juice.
Hot cakes, pancakes: Shoe soles.
Onions: Skunk eggs.
Pickles: Cowcumbers.
Sausages: Sassengers.
Soda pop: Belly wash.
Sweet potatoes: Music roots.
Water: Earth juice. Sky juice.

## Fooling Around

Kicking the wind. Pirooting. "I spent the whole day kicking the wind, just pirooting around."

## Foolish Person

Barrelhead. Cabbagehead. Chowderhead. Dodunk. Foozle. Gooby. Sardine. Yack.

Rhyme about a foolish person:
> The biggest foozle I ever did see
> Was a man what lived in Tennessee.
> He put his shirt on over his coat,
> And buttoned his trousers around his throat.

## Foolish Talk, Nonsense

Flapdoodle. Rimble-ramble. Zizzaparoola.

## to Forget

To disremember. "I just disremembered what I forgot."

## Friend

Old horse. Old socks. "Why, old hoss, what brings you hyar?"

## FRIGHTENED

Streaky. "A man needn't be ashamed to feel a little streaky, not when his mules is about to give out and a pack of wolves is howlin' around him."

## FULL

Really full: Cram-jam-full.

43

# G

## GALLIWAMPUS

"The galliwampus, it's the thing that hollers 'willy-wallo' up in the ellum trees. . . ."

"No, it ain't, Mustang. Them galliwampuses has fins on their backs, and eighteen toes. This here is a hicklesnifter."

## GAMBLER

Gazaboo.

## GARBAGE, JUNK

Orts. Sculch.

## GHOST

Witherlick. Yap.

## GIRL

Nimshy (pronounced nim-shee).

## GLOOMINESS

The dismals. "I've got the dismals."
Gloomiferous. "He looked as gloomiferous as death."

## GLOOMY PERSON

Sulkington.


## TO HAVE A GOOD TIME

To frolicate.


## GRAVEYARD

Bone orchard. Skeleton park.

## GREETINGS

"Why, halloa! I ain't seen you since the hogs et up my brother."

## A GROUCH

Crab-turtle.

## GROUCHY

Pudgetty. "That old crab-turtle, he is as pudgetty as can be."

## GUITAR

Git-flip.

## GUN

Lead chucker. Lead pusher. Manstopper. Murder machine. Peacemaker. Persuader.

Sometimes a gun's owner also gave it a personal name like "Bucksmasher," "Killdevil," or "Old Betsy."

Also see Bullet.

# H

## HAND

Hoof. Paw. "You dingdonged old wally walloo, give us your hoof!"

## HAPPY

To make somebody happy: To put fat on his or her ribs. When you are feeling really happy, call out: "Horse fly!" Also see Laughter.

## HAT

Conk cover.
("Conk" is a
word for nose.)

## HEAD

Knowledge box. Noodlekin.
Also see School.

## HEADACHE

Bust-head.

## HOPELESS CASE

A gone coon (a raccoon with no hope of escape). A gone
goose. A gone possum. "It's all up now. I am a gone
coon."

## HORRIBLE

Monstracious.

# I

## I, Me

When referring to yourself: This child. This horse. "This child is goin' to town."

## Important Person

Big bug. Big toad. Ripstaver. "She is a very big toad hereabouts, a real ripstaver."

## Impossible

"Nobody could do that. It's like scratching your ear with your elbow."

## Insect

Clinker.

## Insults

"You are lower than a hog's belly."

"You are so low you have to look down to look up."

"You are so ignorant, you couldn't drive nails into a snowbank. You couldn't teach a hen to cluck."

"If brains were dynamite, you wouldn't have enough to blow your nose."

These were standard insults. But people also made up their own. They would think of the worst things they could say about somebody, then string them together like this:

"You nasty, yellow-bellied, sneakin', lyin', pestiliferous scorpion!"

"You monstracious, cockeyed, good-for-nothing, snaggletoothed gaub of fat!"

"You egg-suckin', sheep-stealin', toad-eatin', frog-hearted, flop-eared groundhog!"

"You filthy, turtle-backed, snake-headed, bowlegged ton and a half of soap grease!"

Also see Stupid Person.

## INTELLIGENT

"She is so bright you have to look at her through sunglasses."

# Jail

Calabooza. "There I sat in that infernal calabooza playing checkers with my nose."

# K

## KILLER
Corpse-maker.

## KNEES
Hunkers.

# L

## LARGE AMOUNT

Chumblechooks. Scadoodles. Slathers. "He swallowed those eels by the chumblechooks."
Also see Small Amount.

## Laughter

To giggle: To tumble into the Tee-Hee's nest.
To laugh really hard: To break your puckering string.
To try not to laugh: To have the dry grins.

## Lazy Person

A do-little.

## to Leave Fast

To cut dirt. To scallyhoot. " 'Now, you just cut dirt,' he said. 'Don't let me see you round here any more.' So I took my foot in my hand and lit out for home."

## TO LEAVE SECRETLY, TO DISAPPEAR

To absquatulate. "He absquatulated, vamoosed, and cleared out."

## LEGS

Get-alongs. Trotters. Walkers. "I seed clearly that I'd have to try my trotters."

## LOST

"You'll never find it, Mustang. It's like lookin' for a whisper in the wind."

## LOUDMOUTH

Slangwhanger.

## LOVE TALK

To try to get a girl to love you: To court her. To ride herd on her. To sweethearten her. "I sweetheartened her for a whole year, but she got tired of it."

Rhyme to use if you get tired of being sweetheartened:
    I hain't not yours,
    I shan't not be,
    So don't you come
    Arter me.

A steady boyfriend: Yahoo. "He's my yahoo!"

A steady girl friend: Bussy. "She's my bussy!"

Kissing and hugging: Lallygagging. "He and she was lallygagging the whole 'tarnal time."

To get married: To jump the broomstick.

Love stories:

When Ben Harding went to call on Betsy Buzzard, he found another fellow there. He said, "Stranger, do you make purtensions to this gal?" Well, one thing led to another, and they got to fighting. Watching all this, Betsy took a notion on Ben. So she jumped astraddle the other fellow's back and pounded him over the head with a rock until he ran off. Then she and Ben rode away, and they got married the next week.

Bill Wallis was so ugly that when he first got married his wife couldn't bring herself to kiss him. She wanted to, but she just couldn't do it. So finally she took steps.

As Bill told it, "We had this one-horned cow. And one day I went out to the cow lot, and there was my woman with her, cuttin' up all sorts of shines.

"Sez I, 'What are you up to, old woman?' So she told me she'd been practicin' kissin' on that cow. She thought that if she could kiss her, she could kiss me.

" 'Well,' sez I, 'hang the cow! Jest shet your eyes and hold your breath and try it.' Upon that she kissed me so hard you might a-heard it a quarter mile away. And since then nobody's had better kissin' than me!"

## LYING

"If I am lying, may I be kicked to death by grasshoppers."
Also see To Fib.

61

# M

## MEAN, NASTY

"He is mean enough to bite himself."

## MEAN PERSON

Hateful. Snitch. Wart.

## MEDICINE

Spooju.

## MIND YOUR OWN BUSINESS

Skin your own skunk.

## Money

Dooteroomous. Ready John. Rowdy. Spondulix. Swap grease.

Paper money: Frogskins. Shinplasters.

Coins: Buttons. Clinkers. Horse nails. Mint drops.

## Mouth

Bazoo. Dining room. Fly trap. Potato trap.

A wonderful mouth:

Nance Bowers could eat with one corner of her mouth, whistle with the other corner, frown with her upper lip, and smile with her lower lip, all at the same time. But her mouth was so big, she was afraid to laugh very hard. She did that once, and her head fell off.

## to Move Fast

To split the wind.

# N

## NAKED

Shucked.

## NEAT AND CLEAN

Spick and spandy.

## NERVOUSNESS

Peedoodles. "All day long I had the peedoodles."
To be wadgetty. "I was so wadgetty, I couldn't pour cider out of a boot."
To make somebody nervous: To give him or her the flitflats.

## NICE

Slick as a greased pig.
Someone really nice: A dingclinker.

## NOISE

Clatteration. "I give a keen holler and away they went scootin' for the river. You never heard such a clatteration afore."

## NOISES

| | |
|---|---|
| Co-bim! | Ker-slam! |
| Co-chunk! | Ker-slap! |
| Co-wallop! | Ker-slash! |
| Ka-junk! | Ker-slosh! |
| Ka-lump! | Ker-slung! |
| Ker-dash! | Ker-slush! |
| Ker-diff! | Ker-souse! |
| Ker-plunk! | Ker-splash! |

"Down we went in a pile—co-wallop!—bustin' the barrel all to flinderations, nairly shockin' my gizzard out."

## NOSE

Conk. Root. Smeller. Snoot.

## NOSY

Briggity (pronounced bridge-itty).

# O

### Obnoxious Person

Fribble. "You are the biggest fribble in this town."

### Okay

Rusky.

### Ouch!

Otzickity!

# P

## PANTHER

Painter. "Why, stranger, my father swum across that river in a storm with a dead painter in his mouth and a live alligator full splurge after him."

## A Party

Fandango. Frolication.

## Be Patient

Hold your potato. "Just hold your 'tater, now. I'm comin'
quick as I can."

## Peculiar, Unusual

Seldom. "There is something seldom about that horse."

## People

See Banjo Player, Bully, Cook, Coward, Dentist, Doctor, Friend, Gambler, Girl, Grouch, I, Killer, Loudmouth, Preacher, Schoolteacher, Sneak, Woman, Young Person.

To describe someone, also see Angry, Bald-headed, Big, Boastful, Clumsy, Conceited, Confused, Dirty, Dishonest, Dizzy, Dressed Up, Embarrassed, Excited, Fast, Fat, Fierce, Foolish, Frightened, Gloomy, Grouchy, Happy, Hopeless, Hungry (under Eating Talk), Important, Intelligent, Lazy, Lying, Mean, Naked, Neat and Clean, Nervous, Nice, Nosy, Obnoxious, Peculiar, Pretty, Proud, Rich, Rowdy, Sick, Sleepy, Small, Softhearted, Special, Splendid, Strange, Strong, Stubborn, Stupid, Surprised, Talkative, Terrific, Tired, Ugly, Uncertain, Wonderful, Worried, Worthless.

## Perfume

Foo foo. "When she got that foo foo on, you could smell her two miles away."

## Pig

Fin-fum-farum.
A person who cannot resist stealing pigs: Kleptopigiac.

Riddle about a pig:

> As I was a-goin' up stim-stum-starum,
> I met a high giggly-gum-garum
> Carryin' off my fin-fum-farum.
> I said, "I wish I had my gish-mon-garum.
> I would show that giggly-gum-garum
> About carryin' off my fin-fum-farum!"

What does all this mean? See page 109.

## POSSESSIONS

Plunder. "So I packed up all my plunder—my gun, my blanket, my clothes—and I hit the high lonesome, and I never went back."

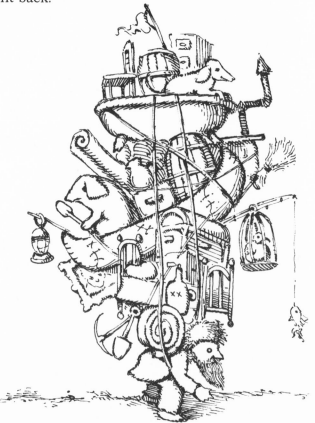

## a Prank

A ding-do.

## Preacher

Sin-buster.

## Pretty

"Pretty as a new-laid egg."
"Pretty as a speckled pup under a red wagon."
"Pretty as a spotted pony."

## Proud

"Proud as a lizard with two tails."

## Quiet

"It was so quiet you could hear
the temperature drop
and the night fall
and day break."

# R

## TO REFUSE

"No, thank you. I would rather kiss a pig."

## Restaurant

A nose bag.
Also see Eating Talk, Food and Drink.


## Rich Person

Rumbustigator.


## Road

"That road is so crooked, you can't tell if you're goin'
somewhere or comin' back home."

### ROUND

Circledicular.

### ROWDY

Rampageous.

### RUCKUS, RUMPUS

Conbobberation.

### TO RUN

To pull foot.

## Scarce

"Scarce as feathers on a snake."

## A School

Knowledge box.

## Schoolteacher

Wisdom-bringer.

## To Show Off

To spread the mustard.

## Sickness

"I feel like I've been shot at and missed."
"I feel like I've been drawn through a knothole."
"I'm low as a toad."
"I'm just breathin', and that's all."
"Powerful sorry you're enjoying such poor health."
Also see Headache, Stomachache.

## Skunk

Perfume factory.

## Sleepy

Snoriferous.

## Small

Knee-high to a bumbly bee. Knee-high to a huckleberry, a toadstool, a milk stool.

## Small Amount

A snitch. (This is also a word for a mean person.)

## Small Room

"That room was so small it wasn't big enough to cuss a cat in."

## Snake

Sarpint.

## SNALLYGASTER

People who have seen a snallygaster say it has four legs, two wings, and a giant beak. It looks something like a big bird. After dark, snallygasters fly through the countryside carrying off horses, cows, and other animals. If they see any children out, they swoop down and try to scare them.

Sometimes a snallygaster will get into a house and take whatever catches its eye, even a refrigerator or a

sofa. But it moves so fast nobody realizes it was there. While the owners are wondering where the missing object went, the snallygaster leaves it in another room or on the roof or in some other unexpected place.

Some people say a snallygaster is not a bird, but a ghost who enjoys fooling around. The best protection against it is to paint a seven-pointed star on the side of your house or barn.

## A Sneak

Slink. "He is not only a killcow, he is a slink."

## Softhearted

"She is so softhearted, she won't whip cream or beat eggs or crack a smile or smack her lips."

## Sounds

See Noises.

## A Special Person or Thing

A few. "He is a few. Well, he is. How he can whip 'em! How he can sw'ar! Whew!"

## Splendid

Splendacious. Splendiferous. "She has the widest mouth you ever saw, and when she grins it is a splendacious sight."

## to Steal

To fraggle.
Also see Pig—A person who cannot resist stealing pigs.

## the Stomach

The digestion.

## Stomachache

Collywobbles.

## Strange

Queerisome.

## a Strange-looking Thing

A do-funny. "Look at that do-funny over there."

## Strong

Robustious.

## Strong Talk

If you are annoyed or angry:
"Blood and massacree-ation!"
"Bugbite and moonshine!"
"By ginger!"
"By grabs!"
"By gravy!"
"By the great hornspoon!"
"By scissors!"
"Dognation!"
"Great crawlin' snails!"
"Great Kezar's ghost!"
"Jumpin' blue blazes!"
"Oh, my stars and possum dogs!"
"Scissorfactions!"
"Snakes and kuckleburrs!"
"Sufferin' cats!"
"Thunder and potatoes!"

If you are surprised:
"I'll be Jimjohned!"
"I'll be a suck-egg mule!"

If you don't believe what
somebody has told you:
"Fidgety-fudge!"

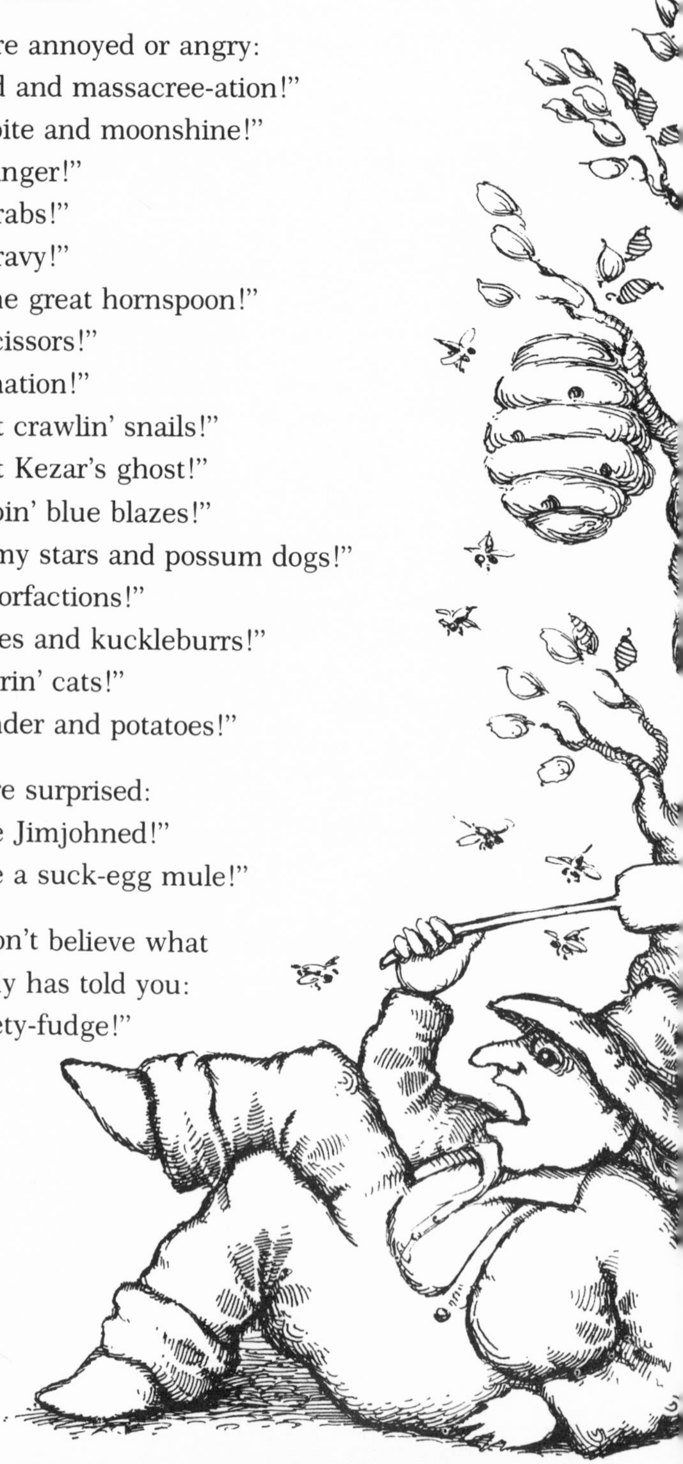

## STUBBORN

Muleiferous.

## STUPID PERSON

"His upper story
must be for rent."

"He has no more sense
than a boiled egg."

Also see Insults.

## FOR SURE, FOR CERTAIN

"Sure as a goose goes barefoot."
"Sure as meat'll fry."
"Sure as snakes crawl."
"Sure as a wheel is round."
"We'll beat 'em. Sure as a goose goes barefoot, we will."

## SURPRISED

Rumguzzled.
Pleasantly surprised: Discumgalligumfricated.
Also see Strong Talk.

# T

## TALK

See Eating Talk, Everyday Talk, Fighting Talk, Foolish Talk, Insults, Love Talk, Strong Talk, Tall Talk, Tough Talk, Visiting Talk.

## TALKATIVE PERSON

Busy lip.

## TALKING CONTEST

Aurgurin' match.

This was a contest between two cowboys to see who could talk the longest. Whether they made any sense didn't matter. They sat cross-legged on the ground facing each other, talking at the same time as fast as they could until one finally ran out of words and wind.

## TALKING A LOT

Rattling your teeth. Wagging your chin. Wagging your tongue at both ends.

## TALL TALK

When a man talked tall he was bragging in a big way about how strong he was and how good he was at fighting and hunting and such things. Usually these brags were wild lies that were supposed to scare whoever was listening half to death. On the frontier and in the backwoods you heard quite a bit of this talk. Sometimes it sounded like this:

"I'm a Salt River roarer! I'm a ring-tailed squealer! I'm a reg'lar screamer from ol' Massassip! I'm half wild horse and half cockeyed alligator, and the rest o' me is crooked snags and red-hot snappin' turtle. I can outrun, outjump, outshoot, outbrag, an' outfight every man on both sides of the river from Pittsburgh to New Orleans. Come on an' see how tough I am! I ain't had a fight for two days, an' I'm spilein' for exercise. . . ."

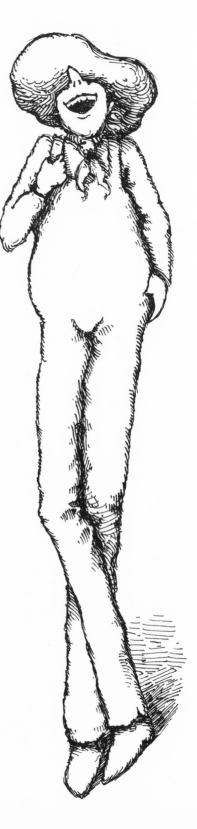

89

Sometimes a speaker got carried away with how dangerous he was.

". . . Size me up and shudder! I'm king of all the eagles and full brother to the b'ars. I'm the bloo-eyed lynx of Whiskey Crossin', and I weigh four thousand pounds! I'm a he-steamboat; I've put a crimp in a catamount [a wildcat] with nothin' but my livin' hands! I've broke a full-grown alligator across my knee, tore him asunder, an' showered his shrinkin' fragments over a full section o' land! I've hugged a cinnamon b'ar to death an' made a grizzly plead for mercy! Who'll come gouge with me? Who'll come bite with me? Who'll put his knuckles in my back? I'm Weazel-eye, the dead shot; I'm the blood-drinkin', skelp-tearin', knife-plyin' demon of Sunflower Creek! Whoopee! whoop! whoop!"

Often all of this was just talk. But if there was somebody else who wanted to fight, there was a standard procedure the two of them followed. They'd strut around and jump up and crack their heels and shout all sorts of things. Then one would puff out his chest and clap his elbows up and down like a rooster flapping its wings, and he'd crow the way a rooster does. Meanwhile, the other would crook his neck and paw at the ground with his feet and whinny and neigh like a stallion. Then they'd strut around some more, and, if they got worked up enough, they'd go after each other.

A genuine badman never got involved in any of this. He talked very little, but when he did he meant exactly what he said.

## Teeth

Grindstones.

## Terrific

Severe. "That is a pretty severe old colt."

## Terrific Person

A horse. A roarer.

A snorter.

A super-terrific person: A ring-tailed roarer. A ripsnorter.

A team of horses. "He is a whole team and a horse extra and a dog under the wagon."

## to Think

To combobbolate. To rumbinate. To wrack your wig. "So I combobbolated and rumbinated and decided to explunctificate my passions with axeltrissity."

This means, "So I thought about it and decided to calm down fast."

## Throat

Goozle.

## Tired

Rumfuzzled.

## to Torture

To cruelize.

## Tough Talk

"I'm a wolf from the woods and I'm on the prowl!"

"When I'm hungry I bites the noses off livin' grizzly b'ars!"

"I am so tough rattlesnakes have bit me and crawled off and died!"

"If you want to die with terror, look at me!"

## A Toy

A happy. A pretty. "Here, child, here is your happy, and here is your pretty."

## Twilight

The edge of night.

# U

## Ugly, Homely

"She is so homely flies won't light on her."
"He is as ugly as a mud fence."

Rhyme about a homely girl:
   The purtiest girl I ever saw
   Was Old Dan Tucker's daughter-in-law.
   Her eyes bugged out and her nose bugged in,
   And her lip hung down over her chin.

## Umbrella

Shower stick.

## Uncertain, Not Sure

"I can't most always sometimes tell."

## to Undress

To shuck. "He shucked off his clothes and jumped into bed."
Also see Naked.

# V

## VERY

All-fired. Desperate. Dreadful. Monstrous. Powerful. Terrible. "The dinner was dreadful well cooked. The food was terrible good. Mrs. Smith was dreadful polite. She was monstrous glad to see you, and I was powerful pleased. It was an all-fired nice night."

## VISITING TALK

Stay a while: "Come in and rest your hands and face."
Sit down: "Put yourself level on that chair."
Don't go home yet: "Stay more!"

# W

**to Walk**

To foot it.

**Watch Out, Beware**

Keep your eyes skinned.

98

## Weather

Heat: "It was hot enough to fry spit."

Cold: "It was cold as snakes."

Fog: "The fog was so thick you could hardly spit."

Drizzle: Spritz.

Heavy rain: Fence-lifter. Goose-drownder. Toad-strangler. "It was just raining down tadpoles. It was a real fence-lifter."

Windy: Blustiferous.

# WHAT'S THAT?

"A whimmy doodle to wind up the moon with."

## TO WHISPER

To shoo-shoo.

## WOMAN

Shemale.

## WONDERFUL

Hugeously grandiferous.

## WORRIED

Doggled.

## WORTHLESS

Not worth shucks. "He ain't worth shucks, and ef you don't lick him for his onmannerly behavior, you ain't worth shucks nuther."

## Young Person

Yearling.

# To Make Up New Words

Here are three ways to make up words nobody ever heard of.

*Add a new ending to an old word.* The ending "-iferous" is a good one to start with. It turns a noun like "mouse" into an adjective you can use to describe somebody or something.

It also gives a word a new meaning. The word "pound" is an example. When you turn it into "poundiferous" it refers to not one pound, but many. When you describe somebody as poundiferous, you are saying he or she is really fat. "Tooth" is another example. When it becomes "toothiferous," it means having a lot of teeth. A person who is toothiferous has more teeth, and bigger ones, than he or she ever will need.

Then there are "snoriferous," "pigiferous," "catiferous," "grandiferous," "splendiferous," "angeliferous," and many other possibilities. After you get used to "-iferous," try endings like "-acious," "-ocious," and "-icular." They work the same way "-iferous" does.

*Turn two words into one.* Take two words or ideas with

103

different meanings. By using parts of each, turn them into one word that stands for both. In this way, "bacon" and "eggs" become "beggs" or "ebac," and "kissing" and "hugging" become "khugging" or "hissing." Here are other examples: To run and jump—to "rump"; to wiggle and twist—to "twiggle"; small and thin—"smin"; big and fat—"bat"; to crouch, then scoot—to "scrooch"; to snoop quietly as a mouse—to "snouse."

A very famous word of this kind is "mimsy." It is a word in *Through the Looking Glass,* a book by Lewis Carroll. Mimsy means miserable and flimsy. "All mimsy were the borogoves," Carroll wrote. Borogoves are make-believe birds—thin, shabby-looking creatures with their feathers sticking out all around like dust mops.

*Make a word out of sounds you like.* Pick out three or four sounds that seem right together and form a word with them. Try "slop," "glop," and "stop"; or "bim," "bam," "bing," "bang"; or "bop," "lop," "sop"; or "zip," "slip," "trip," "trap"; or whatever occurs to you. With the sounds above, you could make up words like "bimbam," "bingbang," "ziptrip," "glopstop," and "glopslop."

Then decide what the word means. An easy way to do this is to describe the picture it creates in your mind. To one person, "bimbam" sounded like an animal with a square head and a boxing glove for a nose. "Bingbang" was a fistfight. "Ziptrip" was a quick vacation. "Glopstop" was a mudhole, and "glopslop" was some really delicious watery stuff you would feed to a hog.

# Notes
# Sources
# Bibliography
# Acknowledgments

# Abbreviations in Notes, Sources, and Bibliography

AS  *American Speech*
DN  *Dialect Notes*
NCFL  *Frank C. Brown Collection of North Carolina Folklore*
NYFQ  *New York Folklore Quarterly*
PADS  Publications of the American Dialect Society
WF  *Western Folklore*

# Notes

The publications cited are described in the Bibliography.

*English and American:* People in the United States speak and write in a dialect or variety of English called "American." "American" differs in several ways from the English language as it is spoken elsewhere. There are differences in words, sayings, spellings, pronunciations, and grammar. These, in turn, have grown out of differences in geography, climate, landscape, plants, animals, the backgrounds and attitudes of the people involved, forms of government, and ways of doing things.

Within the United States, similar differences from region to region have resulted in the development of regional dialects, such as the New England dialect and the southwestern dialect.

The words and sayings Americans use are principally from three sources. One, of course, is the English language that early settlers brought with them. Another is foreign languages. People borrowed foreign words, and then Americanized them, changing their spelling and pronunciation somewhat. At first this borrowing was from Spanish, French, Dutch, and native American (Indian) languages. (The American word "lariat," for example, was taken from the Spanish term *la reata,* meaning a rope or lasso. American cowboys borrowed it from Mexican cowboys.) When immigration from Europe increased, terms from German, Italian, and other tongues were borrowed and Americanized.

The third source, and the most important, is the American

people. Over the years, people in the United States have created words and sayings to meet their needs. They are called "Americanisms."

*Folk speech.* The words and sayings in this book are what folklorists and linguists call "folk speech." Folk speech is informal, colorful, idiomatic language. It has little concern with the rules of grammar, rhetoric, and spelling, and relies heavily on similes and metaphors. Usually it is associated with rural places. But it also is created and used in urban settings by individuals, people who work at various occupations, and members of minority groups and other groups. Of course, this folk speech differs markedly from that in rural areas. See McDavid, *Our Living Traditions*, 228.

*Sartainly, Ain't, Seed.* Many of the examples in the text of how folk speech is used are from sources written in nineteenth-century rural dialect. These dialects are southeastern, mid-southern, and southwestern. Misspellings and grammatical aberrations have been retained, except where clarity was affected.

*Poundiferous* (p. 35): The story of the poundiferous girl is a folk tale that has circulated in the southern and southwestern United States. In the 1940s, it was the basis of a popular song, "Huggin' and Chalkin'."

*Cowcumber* (p. 40): This is how "cucumber" was pronounced in England when the United States was first settled. English colonists brought the pronunciation with them. In the 1950s it still was being used in some sections of the South. See Wilson, *NCFL* 1.

*Zizzaparoola* (p. 42): This is one of five words in the text that are not authentic folk speech. The other four are "galliwampus" (p. 44), "hicklesnifter" (p. 44), "spooju" (p. 62), "kleptopigiac" (p. 69). They appear in the short stories of O. Henry (William Sydney Porter), who coined thousands of words like these during his career. In the sounds they make and the amusing pictures they conjure up, they closely resemble words in the text created by ordinary people. See Cannell, *AS* 12.

*To Jump the Broomstick* (p. 58): Jumping over a broomstick was a marriage ritual in parts of the United States before the Civil War. No clergyman was involved. A broomstick was held a few inches above the floor or the ground, and the couple would hold hands and jump over it. In some cases they would jump twice, forward and backward. Then they were regarded as married. Some Negro slaves were married this way. So were some Creole couples in Louisiana when a priest was not available. The ceremony is related to an old belief that a broomstick will ward off evil spirits at a marriage and provide good luck. See Hand, *AS* 48.

*Noises* (p. 65): To make a noise seem funny, comic writers in the nineteenth century added to it the prefix "ker-," "ka-," "co-," or "che-." In this way, "plunk" became "kerplunk." See Thornton, p. 512.

*The riddle about a pig* (p. 70): The riddle means "Going upstairs I met a bear carrying off my pig. I said, 'I wish I had my gun. I'd show that bear about carrying off my pig.'"

*Knee-High to a Bumbly Bee* (p. 78): In the southern Appalachian Mountains, "bumbly" meant "buzzing." See Kephart, *DN* 4.

*Snallygaster (or Snollygoster)* (pp. 80–81): The principal habitat of the snallygaster seems to be western Maryland between Hagerstown and Frederick. The belief in a bird-monster that carries off people and possessions is related to an ancient belief in ghosts or damned souls who travel through the skies on Hallowe'en or between Christmas and Epiphany and try to take with them any person they encounter. See Spitzer, *AS* 27.

To call someone a "snallygaster" or "snollygoster" was to express disapproval of him or her. President Truman used "snollygoster" to describe politicians who tried to win votes by praying in public. See Pound, *DN* 4; Spitzer, *AS* 29.

*Strong Talk* (p. 84): This kind of talk was a gentle substitute for swearing. Some scholars see a connection between the development of these substitutes and the influence of old Puritan laws that made profanity a crime. Persons convicted under these laws were punished by having their tongues fixed in a cleft stick.

*Tall Talk* (pp. 89–91): Outlandish lies and outlandish language distinguished tall talk from ordinary boasting. Not everybody was good at talking tall, but those who were seemed to talk in three dimensions and four colors.

Tall talk is closely related to the tall tale. Both genres flourished in the United States after the War of 1812, particularly on the western frontier and in the southern backwoods. Life was very difficult for people in those areas, but talking tall about their exploits somehow seemed to make the hardships easier to face.

One heard tall talk from hunters, trappers, riverboatmen, and other rough-and-ready individuals. Backwoods preachers and politicians also practiced the art. They included Davy Crockett, who eventually served in Congress and took his tall talk with him.

Tall talk also was a product of literary invention. Authors and journalists, including Mark Twain, were attracted by the bold, fanciful language they heard, and in their books and articles created their own versions. Most remaining examples of tall talk are from their work. See Thompson, *AS* 9. For examples of the American tall tale in this period, see Schwartz.

*Whoopee!* (p. 90): This was a common exclamation in tall talk. It was borrowed from a call cowboys used in herding cattle and English shepherds used in herding sheep. See Botkin (*A Treasury of American Folklore*), p. 52.

*Mimsy* (p. 104): Lewis Carroll coined a standard term for "mimsy" and other words into which two meanings are packed. He called them "portmanteau" words, after a type of suitcase that was divided into two parts. See Carroll, p. 167.

110

# Sources

The examples of folk speech in this book were used at one time or another during the period 1815 to 1950. They were taken from glossaries, dictionaries of slang, studies of the American language, and early accounts of life in various sections of the United States. They also were obtained from early novels, short stories, poems, and articles.

## Sources of Words and Sayings

Each item is listed below with the region in which it was collected. The regions are designated by the following abbreviations:

NE  Northeast: Connecticut, Maine, Massachusetts, New Hampshire, New York, Rhode Island, Vermont.

MA  Mid-Atlantic: Delaware, Maryland, New Jersey, Pennsylvania.

SE  Southeast: Alabama, Florida, most of Georgia, Kentucky, most of North Carolina, South Carolina, Virginia.

MW  Midwest: Illinois, Indiana, Michigan, Ohio, Wisconsin.

MS  Mid-South, including Ozark Mountains: Arkansas, Louisiana, Mississippi, Missouri, sections of Tennessee.

Ap  Southern Appalachian Mountains: West Virginia; sections of Georgia, North Carolina, and Tennessee.

GP  Great Plains: Iowa, Kansas, Minnesota, Nebraska, North Dakota, South Dakota.

SW  Southwest: Arizona, Colorado, Nevada, New Mexico, Oklahoma, Texas, Utah; southern California.

NW  Northwest: Idaho, Montana, Oregon, Washington, Wyoming; northern California.

Gen  General: Collected in several regions.

OH  O. Henry: From works of O. Henry. See entry "Zizzaparoola" in Notes.

Items are listed in the order in which they appear in the text.

# A

Dudfoozled (MS), bite stumps (NE), eat needles (MW). Varmints (MS). To dingdong (SE). To argufy (Ap). To sumtotalize, to subtotalize (SE).

# B

Onion-head (MS). Box, groundhog (MS). Box knocker, groundhog beater (MS). B'ar (Gen). Gollybuster, gollywhopper (MS). To shoot off your bazoo (SW). Mouth-almighty (NW). Boogeroo, willipus-wallipus (SE). Sand, full of sand (SW); sand on your gizzard (SE). To busticate (GP). Killcow (NE). Lead pill (SW).

# C

Don't fret your pups (MW). To hocus (Gen). Gollumpus, gump (NE). Teetotaciously (Gen). Biggity (MS). Fuddle-britches (MS). Betwaddled (NE), bumfuzzled (SE), golumgumtiated (SW). Bean master, dough belly (NW); gut robber (Gen). Clam-face (SE), possum (SW).

# D

To shake a hoof (SW), to sling an ankle (MS). Dark as a stack of black cats, so dark she couldn't hear herself (Gen). Glopsloptious (NE). Tooth carpenter (Gen). Boongy (GP). So crooked (SW). So dizzy (MS). Pillroller (NW). Bone-cruncher (MW). Slicked up (SW), smooched up (SE), triggered out (MS), like a sore toe (SW).

# E

My belly thinks (MW), my tongue is hanging out (SW). Nose bag (Gen). Messing together (MS). Make long arms (GP), take and rake (MS). Fill your shirt (SE). Padding out your belly (SW). Puckerstopped (NE). To save your bacon (SW). Chin music (Gen), jawbation (SW). Prezactly (MS). All a-twitter (SE), excited as a cat (NE). Lookers (NE). Cheaters (Gen).

# F

Osfrontis (MS). Fumadiddle (SW). Lickety-toot, others (Gen). Poundiferous (SW). Clod-knockers (SE). To woof (SE). Riprocious, savage as a meat-ax (MS). Bustification (MW), squabblification (SE). Scrougers (SE). Pat on the lip (NW). Shuck on the snoot (MW). Ferricadouzer (SW), sockeroo (MW). To blotterate (SE); to chaw up (SW); to exfluncate (SE); to hang up his or her hide, to obfliscate (SW); to rumsquaddle (MS). To sweet-mouth (SE). Cat heads (MS), snowballs (NW). Belly-breakers (SE). Cow paste (MS). Jangle juice (Gen). Hen apples (MS). Nervous salad (SE). Goozlum (MS). Grunt (SE). Bee juice (MS). Shoe soles (NW). Skunk eggs (NW). Cowcumbers (SE). Sassengers (MS). Belly wash (Gen). Music roots (NW). Earth juice (MS), sky juice (MW). Kicking the wind (SW), pirooting (SE). Barrelhead, others (NE). Flapdoodle, rimble-ramble (Gen); zizzaparoola (OH). To disremember (Ap). Old horse (SW), old socks (NW). Streaky (SW). Cram-jam-full (Ap).

# G

Galliwampus, hicklesnifter (OH). Gazaboo (SW). Orts, sculch (NE). Witherlick, yap (NE). Nimshy (NE). Dismals (SE), gloomiferous (SW). Sulkington (MA). To frolicate (MS). Bone

orchard (NW), skeleton park (NE). Since the hogs et up (SE).
Crab-turtle (MW). Pudgetty (NE). Git-flip (MS). Lead chucker,
others (SW). Bucksmasher, others (MS).

# H

Hoof, paw (SW). Put fat on his or her ribs (NE), horse fly (MS).
Conk cover (SW). Knowledge box (NW), noodlekin (MS).
Bust-head (MS). Gone coon (MS), gone goose (MW), gone
possum (MS). Monstracious (Gen).

# I

This child, this horse (SW). Big bug, big toad (Gen); ripstaver
(SE). Scratching your ear (SW). Clinker (MS). Lower than a
hog's belly, others (Gen). So bright (NE).

# J

Calabooza, playing checkers with my nose (SW).

# K

Corpse-maker (MS). Hunkers (MW).

# L

Chumblechooks (SE); scadoodles, slathers (MS). Tee-Hee's nest
(MW), puckering string (NE), dry grins (SE). Do-little (NE). To
cut dirt (SW), to scallyhoot (SE), foot in hand (Ap). To absquatulate (SW). Get-alongs (MW); trotters, walkers (SW). Whisper in
the wind (SW). Slangwhanger (Gen). To court (Gen), to ride
herd (SW), to sweethearten (SE). Yahoo (MS). Bussy (MS).
Lallygagging (NE). To jump the broomstick (MS). May I be
kicked to death (SW).

## M

Mean enough to bite himself (NE). Hateful (MS), snitch (GP), wart (Gen). Spooju (OH). Skin your own skunk (Gen). Dooteroomous, others (Gen). Bazoo (MS), dining room (NW), fly trap (SE), potato trap (NE). To split the wind (SW).

## N

Shucked (MS). Spick and spandy (NE). Peedoodles (Gen), wadgetty (NE), flitflats (GP). Slick as a greased pig, dingclinker (NE). Clatteration (SE). Co-bim, others (Gen). Conk (SW); root (SE); smeller, snoot (Gen). Briggity (SE).

## O

Fribble (Gen). Rusky (MS). Otzickity (SE).

## P

Painter (MS). Fandango (SW), frolication (MS). Hold your potato (MS). Seldom (SW). Foo foo (MS). Fin-fum-farum (MA), Kleptopigiac (OH). Plunder (NW). Ding-do (NE). Sin-buster (SW). Pretty as a new-laid egg (MS), a speckled pup (MW), a spotted pony (NW). Proud as a lizard with two tails (SE).

## Q

So quiet you could hear (MA).

## R

Kiss a pig (MW). Nose bag (Gen). Rumbustigator (SE). Road so crooked (MS). Circledicular (Gen). Rampageous (SE). Conbobberation (SE). To pull foot (SW).

115

# S

Scarce as feathers on a snake (MS). Knowledge box (NW). Wisdom-bringer (SW). To spread the mustard (SW). Drawn through a knothole, shot at and missed, low as a toad (MW); just breathin', enjoying such poor health (SE). Perfume factory (NE). Snoriferous (SE). Knee-high to a bumbly-bee (Ap); a huckleberry, others (Gen). Snitch (MA). A room so small (SE). Sarpint (MS). Snallygaster (MA). Slink (NW). She won't whip cream, others (Gen). A few (SW). Splendacious (MS), splendiferous (NE). To fraggle (NE). Digestion (SE). Collywobbles (Gen). Queerisome (NE), do-funny (MS). Robustious (MS). Blood and massacree-ation (MS); bugbite (NE); by ginger (Gen); by grabs (NE); by gravy, by the great hornspoon (Gen); by scissors (NE); dognation (Gen); great crawlin' snails (MS); great Kezar's ghost (NE); jumpin' blue blazes (NW); stars and possum dogs, scissorfactions, snakes and kuckleburrs (SE); suffering cats (Gen), thunder and potatoes (NW). I'll be Jimjohned, a suck-egg mule (MS). Fidgety-fudge (SE). Muleiferous (SW). No more sense than a boiled egg (Ap), upper story must be for rent (Gen). Sure as a goose goes barefoot (NE), meat'll fry (SE), snakes crawl (MS), a wheel is round (GP). Rumguzzled (MS), discumgalligumfricated (GP).

# T

Busy lip (NE). Augurin' match (SW). Rattling your teeth (SE), wagging your chin (NW), wagging your tongue (MW). Grindstones (MS). Severe (SW). Horse, roarer, snorter (MS). Ringtailed roarer, others (MS). Combobbolate, others (SE). Goozle (MS). Rumfuzzled (SE). To cruelize (NE). I'm a wolf, others (SW). A happy, a pretty (MS). Edge of night (Ap).

# U

Ugly as a mud fence, so homely flies won't light (SE). Shower stick (Gen). Can't most always sometimes (GP). To shuck (NW).

# V

All-fired (SE); desperate, dreadful, monstrous (Gen); powerful (SE), terrible (Gen). Rest your hands and face, put yourself level, stay more (MS).

# W

To foot it (SW). Keep your eyes skinned (SW). Hot enough to fry spit (MS). Cold as snakes (NE). Fog so thick (NE). Spritz (MA). Fence-lifter, others (MS). Blustiferous (Gen). Whimmy doodle (SE). To shoo-shoo (SE). Shemale (SW). Hugeously grandiferous (MA). Doggled (NE). Not worth shucks (SW).

# Y

Yearling (SW).

## Sources of Tales, Rhymes, Other Entries

pp. 18–19  *B'ar story:* From *Mince Pie for the Millions*, Philadelphia, 1846, as quoted in Botkin *(A Treasury of American Folklore)*, p. 24. Adapted.

p. 35  *Story about a poundiferous girl:* Oral tradition.

p. 38  *Rough-and-tumble rhyme:* From *Galveston* (Texas) *Weekly Journal* as quoted in Boatright, p. 1.

p. 41  *"The biggest foozle I ever did see":* Stanza from the folk song "Old Dan Tucker," as quoted in Hudson, p. 493. Adapted.

p. 44  *Galliwampus:* From "Heart of the West" by O. Henry, as quoted in Cannell, *AS* 12.

p. 52  *Method of creating extended insults:* Thompson, *AS* 9; Boatright, p. 153.

p. 58  *"I hain't not yours":* Wilson, *NCFL* 1, p. 516.

p. 59  *When Ben Harding went calling:* From one of a series of comic almanacs dealing with the adventures of

117

Davy Crockett that were published between 1835 and 1856. Quoted in Boatright, p. 42. Adapted.

p. 60   *Bill Wallis was so ugly:* Hooper, p. 41. Adapted.

p. 63   *A wonderful mouth:* "Nance Bowers could eat" is adapted from an account in Boatright, p. 38. "But her mouth was so big" is reported in Loomis, *WF* 6.

p. 70   *Riddle about a pig:* Neal, *NYFQ* 1.

p. 72   *It was so quiet:* Reported by Darcey Dickinson, DeHaven School, Glenshaw, Pennsylvania.

p. 88   *Aurgurin' match:* Adams, p. 10.

p. 89   *"I'm a Salt River roarer!":* Blair and Maine, pp. 105–06. Adapted.

p. 90   *". . . Size me up and shudder!":* Lewis, pp. 273–74. Adapted.

p. 95   *"The purtiest gal I ever saw":* Stanza from the folk song "Old Dan Tucker," as quoted in Boatright, p. 39.

# Bibliography

## Books

Adams, Ramon F., ed. *Western Words: A Dictionary of the Range, Cow Camp and Trail.* Norman, Okla.: University of Oklahoma Press, 1945.

Bartlett, John R. *Dictionary of Americanisms: A Glossary of Words and Phrases Usually Regarded as Peculiar to the United States.* 4th ed. Boston: Little, Brown & Co., 1877.

Bird, Robert M. *Nick of the Woods or The Jibbenainosay.* Revision of 1839 edition. New York: W. J. Widdleton, 1852.

Blair, Walter. *Native American Humor (1800–1900).* New York: American Book Co., 1937. Reprint edition, San Francisco: Chandler Publishing Co., 1960.

Blair, Walter, and Meine, Franklin J., eds. *Half Horse, Half Alligator: The Growth of the Mike Fink Legend.* Chicago: University of Chicago Press, 1956.

Boatright, Mody C. *Folk Laughter on the American Frontier.* New York: The Macmillan Co., 1949.

Botkin, Benjamin A., ed. *A Treasury of American Folklore.* New York: Crown Publishers, 1944.

———, ed. *A Treasury of New England Folklore.* New York: Crown Publishers, 1965.

———, ed. *A Treasury of Western Folklore.* New York: Crown Publishers, 1951.

Burke, T. A., ed. *Polly Peablossom's Wedding and Other Tales.* Philadelphia: T. B. Peterson & Brothers, 1851.

Carroll, Lewis. *Through the Looking Glass.* London: Macmillan & Co., 1872. Reprint edition, New York: W. W. Norton & Co., 1971.

Chittick, V. L. O., ed. *Ring-Tailed Roarers: Tall Tales of the American Frontier 1830–60.* Caldwell, Idaho: Caxton Printers, 1941.

Clemens, Samuel L. [Mark Twain]. *The Adventures of Huckleberry Finn.* New York: Charles L. Webster & Co., 1883. Reprint edition, New York: The Heritage Press, 1952.

————. *Roughing It.* Hartford, Conn.: American Publishing Co., 1872. Reprint edition, Berkeley: University of California Press, 1972.

Colcord, Joanna C., ed. *Sea Language Comes Ashore.* New York: Cornell Maritime Press, 1945.

Craigie, W. A., and Hulbert, J. R., eds. *A Dictionary of American English.* 4 vols. Chicago: University of Chicago Press, 1938–44.

DeVoto, Bernard. *Mark Twain's America.* Boston: Little, Brown & Co., 1932.

Dorson, Richard M. *American Folklore.* Chicago: University of Chicago Press, 1959.

Dorson, Richard M., ed. *Davy Crockett: American Comic Legend.* New York: Rockland Editions, 1939.

Farmer, John S., and Henley, W. E., eds. *Slang and Its Analogues.* 7 vols. London: G. Routledge & Sons, 1890–1904.

Federal Writers' Project. *Idaho Lore.* Caldwell, Idaho: Caxton Printers, 1939.

Flexner, Stuart B. *I Hear America Talking.* New York: Van Nostrand Reinhold Company, 1976.

Flint, Timothy. *Recollections of the Last Ten Years.* Boston: Cummings, Hilliard & Co., 1826. Reprint edition, C. Hartley Grattan, ed. New York: Alfred A. Knopf, 1932. Timothy Flint was a young New England minister who spent the period 1815–25 as a missionary in the Mississippi Valley, then the western frontier of the United States. He recorded his experiences in this book.

Hooper, Johnson J. *The Widow Rugby's Husband, A Night at the Ugly Man's, and Other Tales of Alabama.* Philadelphia: A. Hart, 1851.

Hudson, Arthur P., ed. *Humor of the Old Deep South.* New York: The Macmillan Co., 1936.

Krapp, George P. *The English Language in America.* 2 vols. New York: The Century Co., 1925.

Lewis, Albert H. *Wolfville Days.* New York: Grosset & Dunlap, 1902.

Longstreet, Augustus B. *Georgia Scenes.* New York: Harper & Brothers, 1835.

Masterson, James R., ed. *Tall Tales of Arkansas.* Boston: Chapman & Grimes, 1942.

Mathews, M. M., ed. *The Beginnings of American English.* Chicago: University of Chicago Press, 1931.

————, ed. *A Dictionary of Americanisms.* 2 vols. Chicago: University of Chicago Press, 1951.

Meine, Franklin J., ed. *The Crockett Almanacs.* Chicago: Caxton Club, 1955.

Meine, Franklin J. *Tall Tales from the Southwest: An Anthology of Southern and Southwestern Humor 1830–60.* New York: Alfred A. Knopf, 1930.

Mencken, H. L. *The American Language.* 4th ed. New York: Alfred A. Knopf, 1936. Supplement I, 1946. Supplement II, 1948.

Pickering, John, ed. *A Vocabulary or Collection of Words and Phrases Which Have Been Supposed To Be Familiar to The United States of America.* Boston: Cummings & Hilliard, 1816.

Porter, William T., ed. *A Quarter Race in Kentucky, and Other Sketches.* Philadelphia: Carey & Hart, 1847.

Randolph, Vance, and Wilson, George P. *Down in the Holler: A Gallery of Ozark Folk Speech.* Norman, Okla.: University of Oklahoma Press, 1953.

Rourke, Constance. *American Humor: A Study of the National Character.* New York: Harcourt, Brace & Co., 1931. Reprint edition, New York: Harcourt, Brace, Jovanovich/Harvest Books, 1959.

———. *Davy Crockett.* New York: Harcourt, Brace & Co., 1934.

Ruxton, George Frederic. *Life in the Far West.* New York: Harper & Brothers, 1849. Reprint edition: Leroy R. Hafen, ed. Norman, Okla.: University of Oklahoma Press, 1951. George Ruxton was an English adventurer and author. His *Life in the Far West* was the first reliable account of life among trappers and hunters in the Rocky Mountains before the region was settled.

Schele de Vere, Maximilian, ed. *Americanisms: The English of the New World.* New York: Charles Scribner & Co., 1872.

Schwartz, Alvin. *Whoppers: Tall Tales and Other Lies.* Philadelphia and New York: J. B. Lippincott Co., 1975.

Taliaferro, H. E. ["Skitt"]. *Fisher's River (North Carolina): Scenes and Characters.* New York: Harper & Brothers, 1859.

Taylor, Archer. *A Dictionary of American Proverbs and Proverbial Phrases.* Cambridge: Harvard University Press, 1958.

Thornton, Richard H. *An American Glossary.* 2 vols. London: Francis & Co., 1912.

## Articles

Adkins, Nelson F. "Early Americanisms." *AS* 8 (1933):75–76.

Allan, Philip F. "A Sample of New Hampshire Dialect." *PADS* 15 (1951):65–68.

Allen, Frederick D. "Contributions to the New England Vocabulary." *DN* 1 (1890):18–20.

Ayers, Lucille, and others. "Expressions from Rural Florida." PADS 14 (1950):74–78.

Babcock, Merton. "A Word-List from Zora Neale Hurston." PADS 40 (1963):1–38. Zora Hurston was a twentieth-century black southern folklorist, anthropologist, and novelist.

Bennett, Jacob. "George Savary Wasson and the Dialect of Kittery Point, Maine." AS 49 (1974):54–66. George Wasson was a short-story writer in the period 1900–10 who used the Kittery Point dialect in his work.

Berry, Edward. "Sawmill Talk." [From Texas] AS 3 (1927):24–25.

Bey, Constance, and others. "A Word-List from Missouri." PADS 2 (1944):53–62.

Boroff, David. "A Study of Reformatory Argot." [From New York] AS 26 (1951):190–95.

Braddy, Haldeen. "Tall Talk of the Texas Trans-Pecos." AS 15 (1940):220–22.

Bradley, F. W. "A Word-List from South Carolina." PADS 14 (1950):3–73.

Cannell, Margaret. "O. Henry's Linguistic Unconventionalities." AS 12 (1937):275–83.

Carr, J. W. "A List of Words from Northwest Arkansas." DN 3 (1905):68–101.

———. "A List of Words from Northwest Arkansas." DN 3 (1906):124–65.

———. "A Word-List from Hampstead, N.H." DN 3 (1907):179–204.

Chase, George D. "Word-Lists from Maine." DN 4 (1913):1–6.

Combs, Josiah. "A Word-List from the Southern Highlands." PADS 2 (1944):17–23.

Criswell, E. H. "The Language of the Ozarks." AS 28 (1953):287.

Davison, Zeta C. "A Word-List from the Appalachian and the Piedmont Areas of North Carolina." PADS 19 (1953):8–14.

Dennis, Leah H., and others. "Word-Lists from the South." PADS 2 (1944):6–16.

Dingus, L. R. "A Word-List from Virginia." *DN* 4 (1915):177–93.

———. "Appalachian Mountain Words." *DN* 5 (1927):468–70.

Dondore, Dorothy. "Big Talk." *AS* 6 (1930):45–55.

England, G. A. "Rural Locutions of Maine and Northern New Hampshire." *DN* 4 (1914):67–83.

Farr, T. J. "Folk Speech of Middle Tennessee." *AS* 11 (1936):275–76.

———. "The Language of the Tennessee Mountain Regions." *AS* 14 (1939):89–92.

Hand, Wayland D. "Folk Beliefs and Customs Underlying Folk Speech." *AS* 48 (1973):67–76.

Hanford, G. L. "Metaphor and Simile in American Folk Speech." *DN* 5 (1922):149–80.

Hanley, O. W. "Dialect Words from Southern Indiana." *DN* 3 (1906):113–23.

Hayden, Marie G. "Terms of Disparagement in American Speech." [From Nebraska] *DN* 4 (1915):194–223.

Hogan, Charles H. "A Yankee Comments on Texas Speech." *AS* 20 (1945):81–84.

Kephart, Horace. "A Word-List from the Mountains of North Carolina." *DN* 4 (1917):407–19.

Laughlin, Hugh C. "A Word-List from Buncombe County, North Carolina." PADS 2 (1944):24–27.

Loomis, C. Grant. "Jonathanisms: American Epigrammatic Hyperbole." *WF* 6 (1947):211–27.

McAtee, W. L. "Gleanings from the Dialect of Grant County, Indiana." PADS 15 (1951):51–64.

McDavid, Ravin I., Jr. "Folk Speech." *Our Living Traditions: An Introduction to American Folklore.* Tristram P. Coffin, ed. New York: Basic Books, 1968, pp. 228–37.

McDavid, Ravin I., Jr., and McCord, Virginia G. "The Relationship of the Speech of the American Negro to the Speech of the Whites." [From South Carolina] *AS* 26 (1951):3–17.

Meredith, Mamie. "Tall Talk in America Sixty Years Ago." *AS* 4 (1929):290–93.

Mullen, Kate. "Westernisms." [From the northwestern United States] *AS* 1 (1925):149–53.

Neal, Janice. "Wa'n't That Remarkable!" *NYFQ* 1 (1945):209–20.

Nixon, Phyllis J. "A Glossary of Virginia Words." PADS 5 (1946):9–43.

Payne, L. W., Jr. "A Word-List from East Alabama." *DN* 3 (1909):343–91.

Perkins, Anne E. "Vanishing Expressions of the Maine Coast." *AS* 3 (1927):134–41.

Pound, Louise. "Dialect Speech in Nebraska." *DN* 3 (1905):55–67.

———. "A Second Word-List from Nebraska." *DN* 3 (1912):541–49.

———. "Word-List from Nebraska (III)." *DN* 4 (1916):271–82.

———. "Some Folk Locutions," *AS* 17 (1942):247–50.

Pugh, Delia H. "Some Expressions Heard in New Jersey." *AS* 29 (1954):228.

Randolph, Vance. "A Fourth Ozark Word-List." *AS* 8 (1934):47–53.

Randolph, Vance, and Clemens, Nancy. "A Fifth Ozark Word-List." *AS* 11 (1936):314–18.

Riordan, John L. "Some 19th-Century Frontier Farm Talk." *AS* 27 (1952):290–91.

Rollins, Hyder E. "A West Texas Word-List." *DN* 4 (1915):224–30.

Rupenthal, J. C. "A Word-List from Kansas." *DN* 4 (1916):319–31.

Spitzer, Leo. "Snallygaster." *AS* 27 (1952):237–38.

———. "A Further Note on Snollygoster." *AS* 29 (1954):85.

Steadman, J. M., Jr. "A North Carolina Word-List." *DN* 5 (1918):18–21.

Stevens, James. "Logger Talk." [From the northwestern United States] *AS* 1 (1925):134–40.

Taylor, Jay L. B. "Snake County Talk." [From Missouri] *DN* 5 (1923):197–225.

Thompson, William F. "Frontier Tall Talk." *AS* 9 (1934):187–98.

Tidwell, James N. "A Word-List from Texas." PADS 11 (1949):3–15.

Van Den Bark, Melvin. "Nebraska Pioneer English." *AS* 7 (1933):161–71.

Warner, James H. "A Word-List from Southeast Arkansas." *AS* 13 (1938):3–7.

Warnock, Elsie. "Terms of Approbation and Eulogy in American Dialect Speech." [From Nebraska] *DN* 4 (1913):13–25.

———. "Terms of Disparagement in the Dialect Speech of High School Pupils in California and New Mexico." *DN* 5 (1919):60–73.

Whiting, B. J. "A Maine Word-List." PADS 11 (1949):28–37.

Williams, Cratis D. "A Word-List from the Mountains of Kentucky and North Carolina." PADS 2 (1944):28–31.

Wilson, George P. "Folk Speech." *NCFL* 1 (1952):506–618.

Woodward, C. M. "A Word-List from Virginia and North Carolina." PADS 6 (1946):4–43.

# Acknowledgments

The following persons and organizations helped me to create this book: the lexicographers, linguists, folklorists, and others whose scholarship was my principal resource; librarians at Princeton University and the University of Maine at Orono, where I conducted my research; Gerald Parsons, reference librarian, Folksong Archive, Library of Congress; Barbara Carmer Schwartz and Elizabeth Owen Schwartz. I am grateful to each.

A.S.

ALVIN SCHWARTZ is the author of many books for young people about folk humor, folk life, and other aspects of folklore. He also has written on such varied subjects as crafts, museums, and urban life. Mr. Schwartz lives in Princeton, New Jersey. He and his wife have four children and two black cats.

JOHN O'BRIEN has a Bachelor of Fine Arts degree from the Philadelphia College of Art. He has illustrated several books for children. Mr. O'Brien has also worked as a lifeguard and plays bass regularly with a Dixie band. He lives in Cinnaminson, New Jersey.